DOGS FOR POLICE SERVICE
Programming and Training

DOGS FOR POLICE SERVICE

Programming and Training

Second Printing

By

SAM D. WATSON, JR.

Lieutenant, Oklahoma City Police Department
Oklahoma City, Oklahoma

CHARLES C THOMAS • **PUBLISHER**
Springfield • *Illinois* • *U.S.A.*

Published and Distributed Throughout the World by

CHARLES C THOMAS • PUBLISHER

BANNERSTONE HOUSE

301-327 East Lawrence Avenue, Springfield, Illinois, U.S.A.

© *1963, by* CHARLES C THOMAS • PUBLISHER

ISBN 0-398-02025-6

Library of Congress Catalog Card Number: 63-9643

First Printing, 1963

Second Printing, 1972

*With THOMAS BOOKS careful attention is given to all details of
manufacturing and design. It is the Publisher's desire to present books
that are satisfactory as to their physical qualities and artistic possibilities
and appropriate for their particular use. THOMAS BOOKS will be true
to those laws of quality that assure a good name and good will.*

Printed in the United States of America

N-1

PREFACE

No breed has gained such popularity and distinction in police work as has the German Shepherd. Its special ability and intelligence has earned this distinction. Progressive police departments have recognized the value of the Shepherd in combating crime. Therefore, the Canine Unit is being integrated as a vital unit in many departments.

This book has been written with a two-fold purpose in mind. It will serve as a guide in building a dog program in a police department which has never had one. It will also show, step by step, the basic principles that are involved. Such items as how to enlist the cooperation of city officials and citizens; how to choose handlers; what records are necessary; how to construct kennels economically and serviceably; how to care for and feed the animal; and, how to transport the animal will be discussed in detail.

The book will also serve as a training manual. Details are given to obedience training, protection work, crowd control, teaching the dog to track and search buildings, etc.

It was found that departments desiring a canine unit were hindered or delayed by the limited information available on the subject.

There are many writings about the German Shepherd, his conformation, care and training as a show dog. Although we appreciate a well-formed show dog, we realize that in police work, temperament and spirit are qualities that demand more attention. A police dog must have a very specialized training.

I want to thank Officers B. R. McDonald and Calvin Stephens of the Oklahoma City Police Department for their encouragement and interest in the writing of this book.

The response and cooperation of police departments in Wichita, Lubbock, New Orleans, Amarillo, Baltimore, St. Louis, Ft. Worth and London, England, has contributed to the validity of the material covered.

I would also like to acknowledge the assistance of Jerry Pendry, Steve Hogan and Calvin Stephens for the illustrations; Sgt. R. D. Brokaw for the photographs; and, the Oklahoma Publishing Company for the frontispiece photograph.

S. D. W.

CONTENTS

PART I
HOW TO ESTABLISH A DOG PROGRAM
IN YOUR POLICE DEPARTMENT

PART II
TRAINING YOUR DOG FOR POLICE WORK

DOGS FOR POLICE SERVICE
Programming and Training

PART I

HOW TO ESTABLISH A DOG PROGRAM IN YOUR POLICE DEPARTMENT

INTRODUCTION

In the following chapters, some of the problems involved in the establishment of a dog program within your department will be discussed.

By careful study and application of the suggested guides, your job may be made a little easier and your efforts more successful.

Chapter 1

HOW TO SELL THE POLICE DOG
PROGRAM TO YOUR COMMUNITY

In many communities, citizens have not been sufficiently informed about the dog and his performance in police work. They are somewhat skeptical, often to the point of being afraid to have what they term "a vicious animal" loose on their streets. To those who are familiar with the history of these dogs, this "just ain't so." A trained dog is less dangerous than most of the dogs running loose on city streets daily. The trained police dog is under the constant control of his handler and only becomes aggressive upon command or in defense of himself or his master.

Selling your citizens on the need for dogs for the protection of their community is a vital step in the building of a successful dog program. Fear is usually based on ignorance so the citizen must be informed of the proven value of dogs in police work and be convinced that the working police dog is not a threat on city streets.

The best psychological approach is to let the citizen sell himself. The opportunity to have an active part in setting up the dog program should be provided. The method of citizen participation has been used successfully in many cities.

A group of interested citizens formulating a "Citizens Committee for Dogs for Police Work" should appear before the governing body of the city with a proposal for the inauguration of a dog program in the Police Department. The following proposal is a suggested guide:

CITIZENS COMMITTEE FOR DOGS FOR POLICE WORK

Item 1—The Need for Dogs

This information can be supplied by the Police Department.

Item 2—Composition of the Committee

The committee should be composed of citizens active in local dog clubs and interested in dogs for police work.

Item 3—The Purpose of the Committee

a. To provide advice and help for the Chief of Police from the viewpoint of interested persons in the dog world. This Committee should not concern itself with the particular items for which the dogs are to be used on the Police Force, other than to strongly urge that they be used intelligently and only for the types of work for which they are peculiarly suited.

b. To work toward the goal of public acceptance of dogs on the Police Force and to ultimately present the program to city government and to urge its acceptance and financial responsibility for the program in the future.

c. To show the concerted effort of the dog community behind the program by raising funds to equip, train, and present dogs to the City for use by the Police

d. Selection of the means of training the dog and handler subject to the agreement of the Chief of Police. This will require investigation of the various facilities for professional training of the dogs, as well as the investigation of the results of the training of the various firms, as exemplified by the products in use in other city police departments.

e. Method of raising monies for the purposes outlined below:

1. Donations from organized Dog Clubs.
2. Putting on a benefit dog ribbon match with the aid of all organized dog clubs in your City. The tickets sold by this group, and other non-related groups, to raise funds will be used to purchase the dogs for police work.

Item 4—Enlisting the Support of Civic Groups in Selling the Program.

Item 5—Proposed Budget
  a. Per Dog
     1. Purchase Price
     2. Training for dogs
     3. Board for dogs
     4. Board for handler
     5. Handler training
     6. Police Dog Outfit
  b. Pocket Transistor Radio
     (to provide communication with the dog handler at all times so he will be available for service while on duty.)
  c. Annual Recurring cost per Unit
     1. Feeding
     2. Medical Care
     3. Replacement and care of Unit Equipment
     4. Handler—Personal Liability Insurance
  d. Salary for Handler
     A one-step pay increase above the present salary is recommended because of the extra responsibility of the dog plus the time spent in cleaning the kennel, grooming the dog, daily training, etc.
  e. In-service training Equipment
     NOTE: The expense involved will vary depending upon the trainer contracted to train your dogs, whether dogs are purchased or donated, where items are pur-purchased, etc.

Item 6—The Program Time Schedule
     Should the Committee raise the necessary funds, the City Government may be approached requesting their agreement for the appropriation of funds to maintain the program following the initial impetus which the Committee would provide.
     It is axiomatic that your program will not be successful until and unless the program can be fully maintained with use

of public funds. Any future enlargement should be done completely at the expense of the public funds and the Committee should not be expected to provide the funds for the purchase and training of dogs in the future.

It is entirely possible that civic groups or dog clubs may provide the City with funds for the initial purchase of replacement dogs. Suitable animals may be offered by individual owners or breeders for donation to your program. In this event, these dogs should be screened carefully as to their possible suitability for this type training.

Prior to approaching City Government, all organized dog clubs in your city should be approached and be given the opportunity to financially support the aims and objectives of the program.

The principal advantages in having trained dogs for police work on a Police Force include the following:[*]

"a. The psychological effect of dogs in preventing disorderly behavior of crowds.

"b. The psychological effect on potential criminals in deterring criminal activity and reducing crime.

"c. The aid to police officers in detecting the presence of and capturing suspects, particularly at night in routine patrol; and, in searching alleys, backyards, enclosed premises and wooded areas.

"d. The protection of officers.

"e. The favorable effect on police relations."

"Perhaps the greatest single contribution trained police dogs make to law enforcement is the psychological advantage they afford the police over potential wrong doers."

"Although the dog's role in police work is primarily preventive rather than aggressive, should a handler be attacked or should he direct the dog to "SEEK", the dog's role immediately becomes one of offense."

"Before launching a dog program, a City should obtain a

---

[*] Quoted from Chapman, S. O.: *Dogs in Police Work.* Public Administration Service, 1960.

legal opinion as to its liability for dog bite injuries and the need for insurance coverage. The relevant statutes and judicial decisions of the particular state should be investigated." "A City must be certain that it has insurance which adequately protects it against liability which may result from using dogs for police purposes."

"Certain principals are essential in the development of a sound program:

"a. The program must be fully supported by public funds.

"b. Dogs and handlers must be carefully selected and fully trained.

"c. Dogs should be kenneled at the homes of their handlers and veterinary services should be provided.

"d. The dog unit should be organized as a specialized unit.

"e. Special transportation and communication equipment must be provided.

"f. The entire force should be instructed in the capabilities and limitations of police dogs and in the use that is to be made of them.

"g. The dog unit and its members should be assigned to specifically defined missions and should operate in accordance with carefully formulated tactical procedures.

"h. Attention must be given to program administration and the maintenance of comprehensive records of performance."

It is anticipated that the average useful life of a trained dog on a police force is six years, following which, replacement must be made.

A similar proposal should be made prior to the donation of funds for trained police dogs and the training of their handlers. At the end of a specified time, City Government should evaluate the program. If they feel it has been of definite benefit to the community, they will then provide for the financing of the program from public funds.

It will be necessary for your Police Department to provide

an officer to serve as liaison between the Citizens Committee, the Chief of Police and City Government.

The program will not develop overnight. Plans must be discussed and formulated before they can become concrete working principles. All the work should be done by the Citizens Committee with the Police Department providing assistance and advice when called upon.

Whatever method is used by the Citizens Committee to raise funds, enlist citizen participation in order that as many people as possible will have a definite part in providing the police dogs for your Department.

Those citizens devoting their time and talent to enhancing success of the fund raising effort should be given public recreation.

Another phase of public participation in the dog program of a police department is the donation of dogs by citizens. Of course, these donars should be recognized publicly either on T.V. or in the daily papers. This makes the program more of a community project.

The method of citizen participation has proven successful in many cities in providing a police dog program as well as public acceptance of the program.

Chapter 2

LEGAL ASPECTS OF A DOG PROGRAM

Y our city should obtain a legal opinion from the City attorney before launching a dog program. The following is a sample opinion:

"In regard to the proposal of the Citizens Committee for Dogs for Police Work referred to the Legal Department, the following should be noted:

1. Correspondence with those cities and towns using dogs in police work indicate that no special laws have been enacted, but have provided that —

   a. police dogs be exempt from the city dog license law

   b. it be unlawful to abuse such dogs or interfere with their duties.

2. Evidently based on the fact that the law of 'governmental function' is not being expanded, many jurisdictions have provided for protection with liability insurance coverage."

It will be necessary for your City officials to pass ordinances concerning the police dogs. The following ordinances may be used as guides:

**BE IT ORDAINED BY THE COUNCIL OF
THE CITY OF** . . . .

SECTION. . . . . . ., Title. . . . . . ., Chapter. . . . . . of the Ordinances is hereby amended to read as follows:

"4.1.04. License Fee. There is hereby levied an annual police regulation and inspection fee for dogs kept within the City of. . . . ., the amounts whereof shall be as ordained in the General Schedule of Fees and Charges for Permits, Licenses and Administrative Services set forth

11

in detail in Title......, provided that dogs used by the Police Department will be exempt from any and all such fees."

BE IT ORDAINED BY THE COUNCIL OF THE CITY OF ....

SECTION 1. That it shall be unlawful for any person to willfully or maliciously torture, torment, beat, kick, strike, mutilate, injure, disable or kill any dog used by the Police Department of the City of .... in the performance of the functions or duties of such department, or to interfere with or meddle with any such dog while being used by said department or any member thereof in the performance of any of the functions or duties of said department or of such officer or member. Any person who shall violate any of the provisions of this ordinance shall be deemed guilty of an offense.

Although there are very few legal problems that will arise from the use of dogs, one of the first that will confront you is the attitude of the Court in cases of the dog biting a criminal who was trying to escape or resist arrest. As you know, the law provides that a police officer may use all the force necessary in making an arrest. Therefore, in communities where dogs are used, the Courts have ruled that when necessary, it is legal to use a dog for assistance in making and maintaining an arrest.

There may be times when innocent citizens are accidentally bitten by your dog. In studying the reasons, nine out of ten cases show it was due to negligence of the handler. Handlers become negligent when they develop the attitude that they know how their dogs are going to react in every situation.

Although the handler may know his dog (and as his master, he certainly should know the dog) it is impossible to foresee all the elements in every situation. As long as the human element is present, each encounter will be different.

When an individual approaches a police-trained dog with

the proper respect, he will not be bitten. Sometimes a person may become frightened and make a quick movement or make physical contact with the handler which the dog interprets as an act of violence. This is the dog's signal to do that which he has been trained to do—protect his master.

It is wise for the handler to draw an imaginary circle approximately ten feet in diameter, keeping everyone out and keeping his dog on a six foot leash. By practicing these basic safety measures, the possiblity of an accident is lessened.

Accidents with police dogs do not just happen. They are caused.

If an innocent person is bitten, he should be taken to the nearest hospital for emergency treatment. Due to the training of the German Shepherd to bite and hold, his bite, although painful, is not severe.

The expense of the treatment should be underwritten by the City.

It is important for the City to purchase personal liability insurance on each dog handler. This insurance will cover such things as accidental bites. It can be purchased from most companies at an approximate annual cost of $9.00 per handler.

The question may arise as to whether the Court will recognize a case when the arrest was made on the use of a dog's nose. Never go into Court if this is the only evidence on which you base your case. If you have additional evidence as a result of the arrest, then do.

OWNERSHIP OF DOGS

The dogs must be owned by your city so the policy and procedure for the use of the animals can be enforced by police officials.

The dogs should not be used for training purposes other than official duties.

They should not be entered in any dog shows.

The handlers should not permit their police dog to be used for stud purposes.

Chapter 3

THINGS TO CONSIDER WHEN SELECTING HANDLERS

Many factors must be considered when selecting your dog handlers. In the hands of the wrong master, the trained dog is a potentially dangerous weapon. The handler should be chosen from the upper 25 per cent of the men in your department as to ability and performance.

Transfer into the canine unit must be on a voluntary and permanent basis.

BACKGROUND STUDY

A study of the past activities of each selected applicant should reveal his temper control, patience, self-dicipline, maturity and neatness. He must have the ability to make quick decisions and the intelligence to evaluate a situation and determine the proper approach.

SERVICE TIME

The men who are chosen for handlers should have been with your department at least three years. Due to the expense involved in integrating another dog team into the canine unit, it is wise that you choose only men who have evidenced job stability.

PHYSICAL CONDITION

The officer must be in top physical condition in order to keep pace with his dog.

PERSONAL INTERVIEW

An officer that requests a transfer to the canine unit should be interviewed and all phases of the dog program discussed with him. He should be familiar with the advantages and disadvantages. He must recognize that the dog will be his constant companion. The feelings and attitudes of the other members of his household toward the dog should be considered since they will help to determine the applicant's success or failure as a dog handler.

COMPENSATION

The handler should realize he will be granted no special privileges. The only satisfaction from his assignment is his knowledge of a job well done. However, he should be raised one step or grade in pay to cover the expense of extra cleaning and replacement of uniform items and to compensate him in a small way for the extra responsibility, time and effort he will be required to give.

WORKING CONDITIONS

The handlers should work a seven hour shift. If you want to realize the full potential of the dog, you cannot insist that the handler care for, feed and train his dog after working a full shift. This also leaves him with the responsibility of spending this one hour with his dog. This should be considered part of his day's assignment.

UNIFORM

The only variation in regular departmental uniform will be a leather jacket. This is recommended for the sake of neatness and practicality. Coveralls should be provided for training sessions and certain assignments.

The answers on the dog handler's application should be carefully evaluated to determine the stability and interest of the applicant. Every time a bad selection is made, it will set your program back and cause a financial loss for your city.

The following is a sample application form for prospective dog handlers:

NAME OF DEPARTMENT
DOG HANDLER APPLICATION

CANINE UNIT   DATE_____

_____

Last name   First Name   Middle name

_____

Age   Race   Height   Weight

_____

Rank   Division now assigned

Married (___)   Single (___   Divorced (___)   Separated (___)

Dependents in household:
Name   Relation   Sex   Age

_____

_____

_____

Can you obtain waiver from wife, landlord, and/or others living in same
household? _____ Neighbors? _____

What is your general physical condition? _____

Do you have a regular part-time job? _____ If so, list hours worked,

where and what kind of work _____

_____

Can you give up this extra job if necessary? _____

Do you own any domestic pets? _____ If so, would you be willing to

give them up if you are selected and it be deemed necessary? _____

Have you ever had any experience with dogs? Yes_____ No_____

What kind? _____

Why do you want to be a dog handler? _____

_____

_____

_____

Chapter 4

PROCUREMENT OF DOGS
AND STANDARDS TO GO BY

There are many ways to obtain good dogs for police work — buy them from recognized kennels; breeding; raising your own; and, donations from citizens.

One of the most successful ways to obtain your dogs is though donations from citizens. This will eliminate the expense of purchase and/or breeding. Many fine animals are available through this method. It will also give your citizens a chance to participate in your dog program and thereby increase the public acceptance of the program.

When selecting a dog for police training, it is suggested that only those who possess outstanding aggressive abilities be considered. Only about fifty per cent of the German Shepherds bred in the United States will possess this trait to the desired degree. While the remaining percentage will protect what is in their home surroundings, they will not possess the ability to protect or attack on command in unfamiliar surroundings.

Certain standards and qualifications must be met before a dog can be accepted for police training. The following is a recommended guide for selection of your dogs:

Breed—German Sheperd, males only. The ideal male is 25 inches in height at the shoulder. The weight of a dog in proper health and flesh condition should average seventy-five to ninety-five pounds. Dogs selected should come close to these size standards.

Condition—He must be sound, sturdy and healthy. He must evidence power and aggressiveness. His coat should be healthy and in a good state of grooming.

17

Age—He may be between twelve and twenty-eight months.

Sex—Male only

Color—No restrictions relative to the color of the animal.

Temperament—He must show evidence of alertness, aggressiveness, steadiness and energy. Animals displaying timid, cowardly actions should be disqualified immediately.

Gun Shyness—The animal should be tested for gun shyness. If a dog shows definite signs of cowardly reactions under gun fire, he should be disqualified.

Diseases—The animal should be given a physical examination by a veterinarian to determine his physical condition, checking him for all diseases. If it is detected by the examination that the dog has ever had distemper, he should be disqualified at once. Distemper can and often does damage the nose to the extent that it is not reliable in scent work.

The veterinarian should also check the dog for hip dysplasia. If x-rays show evidence of this, the dog should not be considered for police work.

There are two methods to use in procuring animals by donation. One, a prepared questionnaire to prospective donors. Have them fill in the questionnaire and return it to you. A study of the answers will many times eliminate the need of sending a man to examine the animal. (See suggested questionnaire on page 19.)

Secondly, send a man to check all animals offered to see if they meet the standards that have been set. He must be very tactful and diplomatic with an owner when it is not possible to accept their dog. Explain to each one that just being a German Shepherd is not enough. Go into detail explaining just exactly why you cannot accept their dog. As you explain, remember that the owner has offered one of his most prized possessions and may be hurt if you don't think his dog is good enough for police service.

If the dog is accepted, it is important that you obtain a release from the owner. You may want to use the suggested release on page 20.

The approach you take in procuring your dogs can be one that will help sell your dog program to the community, if it is done in the proper manner.

CHECK LIST FOR POLICE DOGS

Date _____

Checked by _____

Name of dog _____ Sex _____ Age _____

Owner _____ Phone _____

Address _____ City _____ State _____

1. Appearance
   A. Coat (long, medium, short) _____
   B. Eyes (shiny, dull, inflamed) _____
   C. Approximate weight _____
                            Height   Weight
   D. Size: _____

2. Coat: (dull, shedding, shiny)

3. Expression from slow walk: (springy, elegant, clumsy) _____

4. Expression from run: (low to ground, covering much room) _____

5. Dog on leash of handler. Reaction to movements of
   Thrown object _____ Moving hand _____
   Hard word _____ Whistle sound _____

6. Stranger, moving toward dog (growl, bark, hide)_____
   Move toward handler (attacks, hides, no response)_____
   Fast backing (tries to follow, stays in tension, relaxes) _____

7. Reaction to gunshot: (barks, steps back, hides, attacks) _____

8. What is your whole impression of mental shape? (lively, alert, aggressive, super friendly, listless, reserved, more interested in other animals than humans) _____

9. What is your over-all impression of physical shape? (fat, lean, pure, healthy, unhealthy) _____

10. Last worming date _____
    Rabies vaccination date _____
    Permanent distemper date _____

11. Diseases within the last two years _____
    Injuries _____
    Scars _____

12. Describe any mental or physical disturbances known by you (such as

abused by children, etc.) bad habits and dislikes _____

_____

_____

Delayed — refused (reason)   Accepted

_____   Date_____

_____

_____

Date _____

_____

                        Signature of Agent

DONOR RELEASE AGREEMENT

I, the undersigned, do hereby agree to donate to the _____
Police Department, a male German Shepherd dog.

Name of Dog _____

AKC Registration Number _____

I donate said dog without any obligation or cost to the _____
Police Department.

I fully understand that the aforementioned dog will undergo strict and
intricate training, which will include some of the phases listed below:

        Obedience
        Attack on Command
        Protection of his Master
        Building Search
        Guarding of Prisoners
        Chase and bring down a Suspect
        Jump high obstacles
        Track down a suspect

I further agree to accept the return of said dog, if at any time during
his examination or training period, he fails to meet the requirements of the
Canine Unit; or, if I refuse to accept return of the dog, I fully understand
that the _____ Police Department will dispose of the dog in
any manner the Department deems proper.

_____

Signature of Donor   Date

_____

Signature of Officer   Date
in Charge of Canine Unit

Chapter 5

KENNEL CONSTRUCTION

For economic reasons and for the best results in handler-dog relations, most departments have constructed individual kennel units at the home of each handler. The dog lives and is cared for by the handler there. Care of the dog does not become a financial and time-consuming problem.

The dog's daily habits should be much the same as his master's. For example, the use of police dogs is best utilized during the hours of darkness since these are the peak activity hours. The dog and his handler will be sleeping during the day.

Dogs have a tendency to alert on all noises and sounds and if he is left to sleep in his kennel during the daylight hours, he will not get proper rest.

It is recommended that the handler allow the dog to sleep by his bedside when sleeping must be done during the daylight hours. The large majority of off-duty time, as well as on-duty time, should be spent with his master.

Because of the close relationship that must exist between the dog and his handler, the kennel should not be used as living quarters if you are to have a well adjusted dog. If the dog is to reach his full potential, this close relationship must be maintained.

The kennel construction has been designed to compensate for emergency quartering and for short durations. He should not be left in the kennel area for extended periods of time.

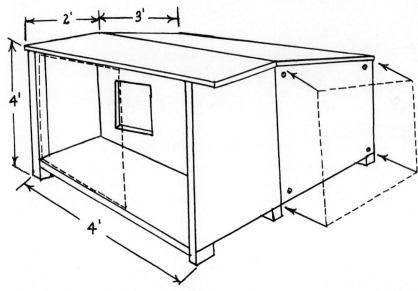

Calvin Stephens

Fig. 1. The frame of the dog house should be redwood two by fours, and the house itself of 5/8 inch exterior plywood. The removable panel on the side of the house can be removed for easier inside cleaning. The panel should be attached by four bolts and wing nuts.

There is a six inch slope from the rear of the porch to the back of the house. The height from the leg to the roof at the back of the house is three feet, six inches. Cover the roof with asphalt roofing material.

In extremely cold climates, walls and floor should be double thickness and insulated.

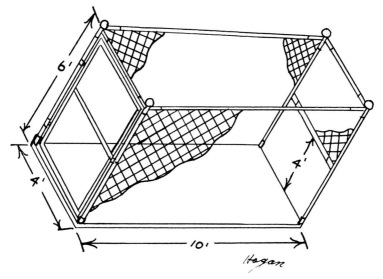

6'

4'

4'

10'

Hogan

Steve Hogan

Fig. 2 4' x 10' x 4" concrete slab with a 2 inch slope for drainage purposes makes the floor of the enclosed dog run. The corner posts are set in sockets so that the pen itself can be removed if necessary. The dog run is enclosed with No. 10 gauge chain link fencing. There is a 4 foot opening at the end of the pen where the dog house attaches to the pen. The gate is 4' x 6' and is located at the opposite end of the pen.

Chapter 6

VEHICLE CONSTRUCTION
FOR TRANSPORTING DOG

It will be necessary for your dog to be mobile. Therefore, you will have to provide a unit for him to ride in. There are many different types of facilities constructed in automobiles, station wagons, three-wheel motorcycles, etc., being used in various departments throughout the United States.

If you use an automobile, it is not practical to use the rear seat. When a sudden stop is made, the dog will be thrown onto the floorboard and injury to the animal could result.

It will be necessary to consider some type of inexpensive, practical construction that will fill the needs and give your dog maximum safety. Following is one method that can be used:

Remove the horizontal portion of the rear seat and build a platform approximately the same level as the rear seat extending from the front of the rear seat to the back of the front seat. Cover this platform with a rug-like material that will be easy to clean.

Attach a chain to the center of the platform that will be long enough for your dog to reach the front seat with his head but not long enough for him to climb over into the front seat.

Attach a shorter chain on the left side of the platform near the side of the automobile. This will enable you to place your dog in a DOWN-STAY position, attaching the short chain to the longer chain and will prevent him from getting up. You will use this when passengers ride with you. The passenger may make a move that your dog would term aggressive, causing him to attack.

24

A screen-type material should be placed over the rear side windows. This will prevent children or curious adults from attempting to pet the dog when he is in the cruiser.

You will note in the illustration that the construction is simple and will not cause modification in the automobile. If necessary, it can be reconverted to a regular cruiser at any time.

The dimensions and expense will vary with the type vehicle used.

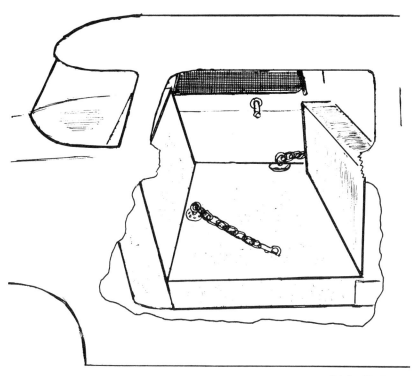

Calvin Stephens

Fig. 3. Cut-away view showing construction of the platform in the rear seat area of the automobile. One-half inch plywood is used. Bracing will vary with the type vehicle used. Use one eye-bolt in the center and one on the left side of the platform. The center eye-bolt will have a thirty-inch chain with a snap on the end attached to it. The eye-bolt on the left side will have a twelve inch chain with a snap on the end. The side rear windows will be covered with quarter-inch hardware cloth.

Chapter 7

GENERAL HEALTH OF YOUR DOG

The importance of continuous care of your dog, kennel and equipment; the proper procedure in checking the health of your dog; feeding and nutrition; and, the necessity of regular grooming is outlined in this chapter.

EQUIPMENT NEEDS FOR THE GENERAL HEALTH OF YOUR DOG

Brush	Comb
Rasp	Canine Toe-nail clippers
Soap	Detergent
Dip	Worm pills
Kennel Broom	Container for stools
Water hose	Metal container for food
Feed bowl	Water pail
Disinfectant	

GROOMING

This should be a time of complete rapport between you and your dog.

Brushing and Combing—Brushing and combing is necessary to remove dead hair, dirt, dust and dead skin. This will give your dog's coat the appearance of being very neat and glossy.

Daily brushing and combing is a great deterrent to skin diseases. This is not a difficult task. You should brush vigorously and in the direction the hair grows, being careful not to brush too hard since this will irritate the skin and cause it to become tender. Your dog will let you know when this happens.

Bathing—Bathing is an important part of your dog's hygiene. The dog will be in the police cruiser with you approximately eight hours a day so you will want him to be as clean and odorless as possible.

It is recommended that you bathe him at least once a month, using any good commercial dog soap, giving all precautions to weather conditions and allowing ample time to thoroughly dry before exposing him to cold or damp air. Before bathing your dog, mineral oil should be placed in his eyes and cotton in his ears.

After you have bathed him, use a dip recommended by your veterinarian. The dip is used to kill fleas and other parasites. It comes in liquid or powder form. Be very careful to follow mixing directions exactly. The dip is poured on the skin area of the dog's body. Be sure to keep it away from his nose, eyes and ears.

Ears—Check your dog's ears daily for an accumulation of wax and/or dirt. In most cases when there is an accumulation of wax in the ear, it can be removed with a cotton swab. If you are unable to do so, take him to the veterinarian.

During the hot summer months, even with proper kennel maintenance, your dog will be bothered by flies on his ears. Your veterinarian can recommend a powder that is particularly effective. If this continues to be a problem, a small amount of a salve, such as Vaseline, smeared on the ear will give some relief. There is nothing that will completely eliminate the bother of the flies, but you can help control them by use of these preventatives.

Toenails—Keeping your Shepherd's nails trimmed is essential to his good health. Use only the nail clippers designed specifically for dogs. Be very careful when you trim the nails in order not to cut them too short. This can cause bleeding. Cutting away only the dead part of the nail is the proper way. It is better to leave the nail a little long than to cut it too short.

After you trim his nails, take a rasp and file the nail much like you would file your own fingernails, using a downward stroke, leaving the nail smooth. If you cut a nail too short and cause it to bleed, do not file it for at least a day or two.

Overgrown nails cause foot ailments, sometimes to the point of lameness. The dog's nails must have proper care.

The dog in police work will spend much of his time on hard surfaces and his kennel floor will be concrete. Usually, this hard surface will control nail growth by the continuous wearing-off action, thereby eliminating much of the nail problem.

Teeth—You should check your dog's mouth regularly for loose or broken teeth. If you detect any irregularities, take him to the veterinarian for immediate care. Bad teeth can become abscessed causing infection to spread to the nose where permanent injury could result, leaving the dog useless for scent work.

Feet—If your dog's feet become sore from being on concrete or hard surfaces, it is recommended that you use a compound such as Toughskin. This will toughen the skin and remove the soreness.

Physical Examination—It is recommended that your dog be taken to the veterinarian for a physical examination at least once a year. Many times, bad health conditions cannot be detected by an amateur.

FEEDING AND NUTRITION

Rules For Good Feeding

Your dog should be fed once a day. This is sufficient for an adult dog. The dog trained for police work should be fed at the same time every day, approximately four hours before he goes on duty.

It is important that you teach your dog to eat the food that is given and to eat it at the time it is given to him. Never leave his food out for more than twenty or thirty minutes. If he does not eat it within that time, take it away and do not feed him again until the same time the next day. This will teach your dog to eat what is given to him, when it is given. This will also prevent the food from souring or spoiling.

A dog will gulp his food without chewing. There is no

digestive process in the mouth. The teeth are used mainly for tearing or crushing his food.

How Much to Feed Your Dog

The amount of food your dog will require is determined by many factors such as age, size and physical condition. Of these, the size of the dog and the work that he is to do is the most important.

The following table may be used as a guide:

Weight of Dog	Amount of Food Daily
50 pounds	2½ pounds
75 pounds	3¼ pounds
100 pounds	4 pounds
150 pounds	5¼ pounds

The ratio of food portions should be 50 percent meat (beef or horsement); 25 percent vegetable (spinach, onions, carrots, tomatoes, beets, potatoes, cabbage or turnips); and, 25 percent cereal. With the exception of beets, carrots and tomatoes, the vegetables must be cooked and mixed thoroughly with the other food or the dog may refuse to eat them.

A teaspoon of vitamin-mineral supplement should be mixed with the meal daily. The diet for an average adult dog may have 10 percent fat content. However, as the cereal ratio increases, so should the ratio of fat increase, not to exceed 15 percent of the total diet.

Many of the commercial dog foods on the market today manufactured by reputable firms are complete and balanced diets. If you choose to use one of these, evaluate them by the statement of the contents and if needed, supplement this food in order that your dog will be properly fed.

Water

Regardless of the amount or type of food you feed your dog, he must be supplied with plenty of clean, cool drinking water.

KENNEL MAINTENANCE

It is essential to good health for your dog that the basic

methods of maintaining and cleaning the kennel are practiced.

Your dog should be healthy, lively, happy and full of life. One of the most important factors in insuring this condition is a clean and sanitary kennel.

The permanent kennel should be kept clean at all times. This is very important because of the small area. Use the following method in cleaning the kennel:

Remove stools from the kennel once a day and place in a special container. Wash the remainder of the stool from the kennel with plain water. Twice a week, scrub all parts of the kennel with soap and water. This includes floor, door, walls, sides and wire fence. Rinse all soap from the kennel. Soap film left in the kennel can cause diarrhea in your dog.

Once a week, disinfect the kennel. The disinfectant must also be rinsed. This process should be followed a minimum of once a week.

The food bowl and water pail must be washed every day.

Check the kennel daily for loose wire or chewed boards that could cause injury to your dog or allow him to escape.

Use cedar shavings in the dog house for bedding. The shavings should be changed every four weeks.

Chapter 8

DISEASES AND HOW
TO CONTROL THEM

When your department acquires your German Shepherd, he should be given a physical examination by a veterinarian. If he is accepted for police service, you will know he is a healthy, strong, adult dog. You will not be confronted with many of the problems concerning diseases and his general health if you will practice good grooming and maintain sanitary conditions for him.

From an educational viewpoint, you should understand the different types of diseases and how to control them, remembering that you are an amateur. When in doubt, take him to the veterinarian. It's better to be sure and safe.

Many of the serious diseases, such as rabies, distemper, hepatitis and leptospirosis, can be prevented by immunization. Your dog must be immunized against these diseases and given a booster shot annually.

Rabies is one of the oldest diseases known to man and it is common to all warm-blooded animals. It is spread through the bite and usually is fatal. This shot should be given annually.

Distemper is a virus that affects all the organs of a dog's body.

Hepatitis is a virus disease and is usually fatal. The disease affects all the organs of a dog's body but the liver is the vital organ most commonly affected.

Leptospirosis is a bacteria and is fairly common in dogs. The organs most affected are the kidneys and the liver. When a dog is affected with this disease, he usually dies.

31

EXTERNAL PARASITES

Parasites that must be guarded against are fleas, ticks and mites.

Fleas and *ticks* are common to dogs and cause a great deal of skin irritation and torment to them. They can be controlled by using a dip which is applied to the dog by pouring it over the skin area.

Mites are small creatures . . . some you can see and some cannot be seen. They cause mange in a dog. This can also be controlled by the use of a dip. There is a variety called the Ear Mite that causes damage to the outer ear resulting in deafness.

It is important that your dog be treated immediately if he contracts a skin disease. In case of ear trouble, take him to the veterinarian.

INTERNAL PARASITES

There are many types of parasites that live inside a dog's body and maintain all their needs from him. They constantly rob him of his blood and essential parts of his diet and interfere with the normal organ functions.

Although internal parasites can cause a serious problem, if proper sanitary conditions are maintained and good grooming is practiced daily, the problem will be of minor consequence.

There are five types of worms with which to be concerned. They are Hook, Round, Tape, Heart and Whipworm. When you first assume the responsibility for your dog's care, have him examined for all types of worms.

Roundworms are very common in young dogs but not of serious concern in the adult dog.

Hookworms are the most common of the internal parasites found in dogs. If they are allowed to go unchecked, they can do great damage to the intestinal lining. The general condition of the dog will often be run-down because of the serious loss of blood on which the Hookworm feeds.

The *Whipworm* is not as common, however it is essential to the good health of your dog to rid him of this infectious worm as soon as possible after detection. The Whipworm causes severe emaciation, rough hair coat and may cause death by perforation of the intestinal wall.

The **Heartworm** lives in the chambers of a dog's heart and interferes with the heart action. It is recommended that you never accept a dog for police service if it is determined by a veterinarian's examination that he has Heartworms, even though proper medical care can cure the animal. Permanent heart damage can result from Heartworm.

Dogs infected with **Tapeworms** lose weight, become dull and sluggish and their coat becomes brittle and dry. This worm can be detected by a substance in the stool that resembles rice. Proper medication as recommended by a veterinarian will cure him.

Protozoa is a small, one-celled parasite which causes disease in the dog. One such disease, coccidia, can cause severe dysentery which could result in the dog's death. Another disease caused by protozoa is coccidiosis. This disease is not as serious and can be controlled by maintaining sanitary conditions in the kennel.

It is recommended that you take a stool specimen to the veterinarian every six months. By examination, it can be determined if your dog has any of the internal parasites. If parasites are present, he will prescribe proper medication. If the medication can be given at home, it is recommended that you do so.

To help control internal parasites, give particular attention to the section on kennel maintenance and practice it constantly and consistently.

SYMPTOMS OF A SICK DOG

Diarrhea, failure to eat for two or more days, intense coughing and/or sneezing, pus discharge, blood in the urine, loss of hair without obvious reason, repeated vomiting, unusual behavior, fever, discoloration of gums or discharge from the eyes are all indications of an unhealthy condition in your dog.

Chapter 9

CANINE FIRST AID

Any injury to your dog, if neglected, can render him useless for police work. It is important that he be checked daily for cuts and injuries or signs of disease if you expect to have a good, healthy animal.

You should know and be able to practice first aid, keeping in mind that first aid is only used as a method of preventing more serious injury or death to your dog.

It will be necessary for your dog to be muzzled before giving him first aid. Dogs often become confused and frightened when they are injured and will bite in self-defense. If you do not have a muzzle available, a belt, rope, shoe string or leash can be used. This is tied around the dog's jaws, placing the knot under the lower jaw.

Bites—Wash the wounded area with soap and water. Remove all hair from and around the wound. Apply an antiseptic and make sure the wound remains open.

Choking—If your dog begins to choke, examine his mouth and throat carefully for particles that may be lodged there. If you do not find anything and he continues to choke, take him to a veterinarian immediately.

Cuts—To stop bleeding, apply a pressure bandage or tourniquet, depending on the severity and location of the cut. If a tourniquet is used, be sure it is loosened every five minutes for an interval of ten-fifteen seconds. If it is a severe cut that requires suturing, take him to the veterinarian. If not, remove the hair, use an antiseptic and bandage when the bleeding has stopped.

Overheating—When overheating occurs, place your dog in

the coolest spot you can find. Wet him with water, especially on the head. Do not let him drink until he has cooled down and then only in small amounts.

Poisons—If your dog gets poisoned, give him something to make him vomit immediately, such as one teaspoon of hydrogen peroxide in one cupful of water, or a tablespoon of salt mixed in half a glass of water, followed by a generous portion of Epsom Salts in a glass of water. Take him to the veterinarian immediately. Identify the poison by name if possible.

Burns—The most common and probably the only type burn you will be confronted with is the flame. In case of this type burn, apply a grease or medicinal ointment to prevent extreme blistering. Speed of treatment is important.

Fits—When in a fit, your dog probably will not be conscious, therefore he will not be dangerous. However, in some types of fits, he will be semiconscious and should be considered dangerous. In either case, confine him and consult your veterinarian immediately.

Poisonous Snakebite—Make a deep cut below the wound. *Do not suck the wound.* If it is a leg bite, use a tourniquet, remembering to loosen it every five minutes for a few seconds interval. If possible, identify the snake and contact your veterinarian immediately.

Shock—When your animal is in a state of shock, it is important to give him artificial respiration due to the paralyzed condition of the respiratory track. Keep him warm and let him rest. Rest is important. Contact your veterinarian.

Broken Bones—Never try to set a broken bone yourself. Apply splints to prevent movement of the broken bone. Splints can be made from such material as sticks, cardboard tied together with your leash, belt or shoelaces. Bones protruding through the skin should be covered with a clean bandage. Take the animal to the hospital immediately.

Chapter 10

RECORDS

There are many types of records that must be kept if your program is to be evaluated accurately. Records on the individual dog will reveal strong points and weak points. Some dogs will excel in tracking while others will show superior performances in crowd control.

These strengths must be known before they can be used to an advantage. The weaknesses must also be known since they will point up the need for intensified training in particular areas.

In the initial phase of your program, you will encounter the question "are the dogs worth what they cost the City?"

Records adequately kept can be concrete proof of the value of the dog program and what it is doing for your citizens. Economic factors fade into insignificance when balanced with human safety, prevention of crime and preservation of peace.

If you are going to sell city officials on the worth of the program, you must be able to produce the facts . . . instances when the dog has deterred crime or helped maintain public security.

Records of expenditures aid in adjusting the budget. On page 37 will be found a suggested record for initial expenditures.

It is necessary that an inventory be kept of all equipment purchased and a record maintained of the items checked out to each handler. The form on page 37 may serve as a guide for such a record.

INITIAL EXPENDITURE FOR ONE UNIT

DOG'S NAME _____ DATE _____

COST

Dog sale price
Board for Dog during training
Cost of training dog
Expense for handler during period of training dog
Cost of Handler training
Work equipment needs for the dog
Kennel Needs
    Dog house
    Chain-link fence
    Concrete flooring
    Cleaning equipment
    Feeding equipment
Automobile Construction
    Window protectors
    Platform in lieu of rear seat
    Chains
      TOTAL COST

CHECK-OUT EQUIPMENT RECORD

HANDLER _____

                 OUT   IN   REPLACED

One kennel unit
Kennel mop
Brush
Comb
Harness
Work Collar
6-foot leash
20-foot leash
Search & Signal light
Water Pail
Food Bowl
Muzzle
2 identification shields
    (for dog)
Clippers
Rasp
Other

It is important that a record be maintained of your dog's health condition. This will also help determine the handler's ability to provide proper care and maintenance.

MEDICAL RECORD

DOG'S NAME _____

	DATE GIVEN	DATE DUE
IMMUNIZATIONS:		
Rabies		
D-H-L		
INTERNAL PARASITES		
Roundworm		
Hookworm		
Tapeworm		
Whipworm		
Heartworm		
Protozoa		
MISC. VET. CARE		
Cuts		
Burns		
Broken Bones		
Other		

A daily activity card should be kept by each handler. From this, monthly and yearly records can be maintained, and the value of the program exemplified to city officials. Special care should be given to this record since it will be the basis of your evaluation. A sample activity card is on page 40.

A record should be kept to determine the dog's ability to perform those tasks for which he has been trained. This ability should be evaluated in a two-hour training session to be held a minimum of once each week. This card should be filled out by the unit supervisor. A sample performance record is found on page 41.

It will be beneficial to inventory all the equipment at your training site and keep a permanent record on file. The following may be used as a guide:

TRAINING SITE EQUIPMENT

EQUIPMENT	NUMBER	TYPE
Hurdles		
Ramps		
Climbing Walls		
Walking Logs		
Window		
Tunnel		
Stairway		
Ladder		
Water Jump		

Keep a record of the donor's release agreement. See Chapter 4 for example.

Keep a record of the handler's application forms for use in selecting new handlers. It should be a known fact in your Department that anyone interested in working as a handler will be considered.

It will be necessary for the supervisor of the unit to study the records of other divisions such as the burglary detail, armed robbery, etc. for the purpose of selective enforcement so the dogs may be used where they will be of the greatest service.

OFFICER'S FIELD ACTIVITY REPORT

K-9   **K-9**

OFFICER'S NAME _____ DATE _____

DOG'S NAME _____ DISTRICT _____

Hours Worked_____ Time Out_____ Time In_____ Auto Equip. #_____

TYPE CALL	NO.	ARREST MADE	NO.
BLGD. SEARCH		MISC. ARREST	
A.D.T. CALLS		BURGLARY	
BUSINESS CHECK		ROBBERY	
CROWD CONTROL		OTHER FELONY ARREST	
DISTURBANCE		1.	
FIGHT		2.	
FIRE		TRAFFIC ARREST	
GUN-KNIFE CALL		OTHER ACTIVITY	
HOLD-UP		COURT	
PROWLER		RE-TRAINING	
PED. CHECK		DOG SICK	
RES. CHECKED		ROAD BLOCK	
TRACK & TRAIL			
VEH. CHECKED			

REMARKS: _____

_____

_____

_____

Any arrest made, attach arrest report or detail under remarks.

WEEKLY EVALUATION RECORD

NAME OF DOG _____ DATE _____

HANDLER _____

OBEDIENCE	GOOD	FAIR	POOR
1. Heeling on leash			
2. Heeling off leash			
3. Sit on command			
4. Stand on command			
5. Down on command			
6. Stay in Sit position			
7. Stay in Down position—10 mins.			
8. Stay in Stand position			
9. Jumping 4-foot hurdle			
10. Climbing over 6-foot Climbing Wall			
FIELD PROBLEMS			
1. Retrieving			
2. Handler protection			
3. Stopping fleeing suspect			
4. Crowd Control			
5. Guarding prisoner			
6. Obedience after attack			
TRACKING & SCENT WORK			
1. Working a quarter-mile track			
2. Working a half-mile track			
3. Searching building & finding suspect			

REMARKS OF SUPERVISOR (over-all evaluation of dog and handler):___

_____

_____

_____

CANINE UNIT EXPENSE RECORD

DOG'S NAME _____ HANDLER _____

	Jan	Feb	Mar	Apr	May	June	July	Aug	Sept
FOOD DRY									
CANNED									
FOOD TOTAL									
EQUIPMENT REPAIR									
EQUIPMENT REPLACEMENT									
EQUIPMENT TOTAL									
VET. CARE SHOTS 1. RABIES									
2. DISTEMPER									
3. HEPT.									
4. LIPTO									
WORMED									
MISC. VET. CARE									
TOTAL VET. EXPENSE									
MISC. EXPENSES									
MONTHLY TOTAL									

TOTAL ANNUAL COST _____

Chapter 11

THE CANINE UNIT
AND PUBLIC RELATIONS

The police dog in your Department can be one of your most effective public relations tools if utilized properly.

One of the most important phases of a police dog program is educating the people in your community regarding their relationship to the dogs. A good method is the use of exhibits and demonstrations.

Almost everyone likes to see a trained dog work. It holds a certain fascination for them to see the power evidenced as the dog attacks on command and goes all out to protect his master, and at another command becomes quiet and gentle. Those watching the performance stand in awe of the handler, his knowledge and control, and the ability of his dog. Usually the demonstration viewers are comparing their own dog with the police dog. They come to the conclusion that the trained police dog is a far cry from the unruly, uncontrolled animal they have at home.

Your police department canine unit will have many requests to perform before various civic groups, churches and schools. The type program presented will depend upon the size of your dog team and the number of dogs available for demonstration purposes. A typical demonstration could include two patrolmen-handlers, two dogs and a moderator.

The actual demonstration should include such things as an obedience demonstration; a retrieving exhibit when the dog will seek and fetch; an attack situation when your agitator may use a gun to give added emphasis to the protective ability of your dog; the apprehension of a running suspect; and, using the spectators at a safe distance, a demonstration of crowd control.

As each phase of training is demonstrated, the moderator explains the type training involved and how the particular exercise fits in with police work.

In some instances it may not be practical to have a dog and handler go through all the phases suggested above. There are times when the use of colored slides would be more acceptable by the viewers. A projector and screen can be set up in an area much too small for an actual demonstration. Also, by using the colored slides, the use of the dogs could be explained in greater detail by showing building search, guarding of prisoners and other actual events when the dog assisted in the apprehension of criminals.

Even when using slides and if space permits, basic obedience, an attack and the **out** command could be demonstrated by a handler-dog team.

The moderator should stress the control of the handler over the dog rather than emphasizing the viciousness of the dog.

A demonstration should never last more than one hour. At the close of each demonstration, the moderator should speak briefly on the citizens' role in relation to the dogs, emphasizing these safety points:

1. Never attempt to pet a trained police dog.
2. Never try to touch the handler when his dog is with him.
3. Never try to approach the dog when he is in the patrol cruiser.
4. Never make any quick movements or aggressive actions around the dog.
5. If it is necessary to talk with the handler, stand about ten feet away. The dog will be on a six foot leash and if you should make a move the dog would term aggressive, he would not be able to reach you.

Never use an undependable dog in a demonstration. A

poor demonstration does not create any good will.

Exhibit your dog in the downtown area by having a patrolman walk the street with the dog during peak business hours. Use your canine unit at public events that draw large crowds. This accomplishes a two-fold purpose: it exhibits the dog and his ability to a large number of people; and, the canine unit can do the job of crowd control that would require the services of fifteen or twenty patrolmen.

Anytime a canine unit appears in public, whether for demonstration purposes or on actual duty, all eyes will be on the handler-dog team. Make sure the handler takes pride in the appearance of his dog; that the dog's coat is always smooth and shiny and that he has a well-cared-for look.

The handler should also take great pride in his own personal appearance; that his uniform is always fresh, trouser creases sharp, shoes shined, hat clean, etc.

A handler will have many opportunities during a regular tour of duty to "show off" his dog. He should always be proud of his assignment, even "strut" a bit, but never be arrogant. Arrogance can destroy in a few minutes a good public image that has taken months to create.

Remember, a canine unit will be the focal point of attention any time it appears. Make sure it sells your department to the public each time an appearance is made—whether it be a regular tour of duty or a public demonstration. This will be one of the determining factors in the success of your canine program.

PART II

TRAINING YOUR DOG
FOR POLICE WORK

INTRODUCTION

In the following chapters, we want to introduce you to the German Shepherd in a capacity you have not known him before. We want to instill one word and this word should be kept in mind at all times . . . CONTROL·

CONTROL

As you attain control of your dog, and this can be accomplished only through hard work and patience, you will have one of the most effective weapons ever discovered to combat crime and help provide safety and security to your community.

There are three types of training to which your dog will respond. First, forced training. This he obeys through fear. Second, your dog responds to commands because he knows he will receive a tidbit as a reward. Third, he obeys because he loves his master.

The full potential of your dog's ability is never reached through fear or the giving of rewards. When he responds to your commands because of the love he has for you, he will continually strive to go beyond what you expect.

The German Shepherd has been selected as the breed best suited for police service. This has been determined because the Shepherd has demonstrated the following traits: keen sense of smell, endurance, reliability, speed, power, courage, trackability and ability to adapt to almost any climate.

47

Chapter 12

GETTING ACQUAINTED
WITH YOUR DOG

Your German Shepherd should be strong, alert, well co-ordinated and active.

A male Shepherd, in good physical condition, should be twenty-five inches in height at the shoulder and weigh between seventy-five and ninety-five pounds.

Contrary to what you may have heard and read about the German Shepherd, there will be only approximately half that will meet the standard needs for police service.

In spite of his size and character, the Shepherd is not a beligerent brawler, but with proper training, will be aggressive, protective and under your control at all times. He only tolerates those with whom he comes in daily contact. His devotion belongs to one person . . . his master.

He has many qualities including loyalty, courage and intelligence to retain training. The Shepherd in police service must not be a nervous or excitable animal but exhibit a picture of self-confidence.

The experience you have with your dog will show you he is your most loyal and courageous friend.

As you work with your dog, he will begin to take on your personality. Therefore, it is very important that you always set a good example for him. Don't teach him any bad habits by your words or actions.

As a working police dog, he must display courage; he must not be gun shy; and, he must be able to make use of his nose.

Your Shepherd is an intelligent animal. You must understand him. The problems that arise will not be the fault of your dog but will be due to your lack of understanding. If the bond between you and your dog is sealed with love and devotion, he will be your companion, protect you with his life and be your life-long friend.

A dog's sense of smell far surpasses that of man. Tests indicate that the dog's ability to smell odors is approximately 100 times greater than that of humans. It is almost impossible to comprehend a dog's ability to distinguish specific odors for long periods of time.

Tests have proven that the average Shepherd's hearing ability is ten times greater than human hearing. In one test, the dog responded to a sound at a distance of 180 yards that man could not hear for more than 40 yards.

Conclusive experiments have pointed out that a dog's range of vision is neither as sharp and clear nor as great as that of man. Tests indicate that dogs are very sensitive to movement. When an object within their line of vision moves, they will respond to it. It is not known for sure whether a dog can distinguish color. However, most experts agree that a dog's world is black and white.

The dog's limitation in the field of vision is more than offset by his exceptional sensitivity to sound and odor.

Prior to training your dog, take time to get acquainted with him. Notice his reactions to affection and correction and his willingness to please. Study the animal and determine his potential. Never expect more of your dog than his potential indicates.

An important principle to remember as you train your dog is that *you must have patience*. When you lose patience, you lose control of your dog.

Never rush his training. There will be times when you will see little progress and there will be times when it is apparent you are making great strides. It is important that your dog understands what is expected of him. When he does understand, he will perform as you expect him to and will not forget.

If he does not respond to a command, you can be sure that

you, as a trainer, are at fault. In almost every instance, it is an indication that you have not taught him well.

Repeating a command in training your dog is necessary in order that he fully understand what he is expected to do. If you become impatient and advance to another lesson before he is ready, you will confuse him. A dog does not have reasoning power. They associate the sound of the spoken word with the action you want them to perform. Therefore it must be repeated until it becomes habit with him.

There is a learning limit. If a dog has worked too long in one area of learning, he becomes incapable of further learning during that teaching session. When you notice this limit has been reached, postpone further training until the dog has had opportunity for a change of activity or a rest period.

Knowing the type praise to which your dog will respond is vital if he is to do his best for you. Praise can either be verbal or physical. Your dog will respond to one or both types. Use the one that fits him best.

There must be a distinct difference in your tone of voice when you give verbal praise, issue commands or correct your dog. This must be done with consistency. When you use verbal praise, remember to keep your voice low and soft. Your words must be spoken in a pleasant tone.

When physical praise is employed, pet your dog with your hands. Playing or rough-housing with him is another type of physical praise. This should be done only during breaks, rest periods or at the end of the training session.

Since a dog in police service works six to eight hours a day, he will work best for the affection he receives from his master. Be sure to praise him when he deserves it.

You must be consistent in correction. This shows the dog he has done wrong. Never let him disobey without correcting him. Correct him at the first sign of disobedience.

Timing, consistency and the tone of voice are the most important factors in correction. Never be too severe, strike, kick or hit him with any object.

The German Shepherd you are training is an intelligent, adult animal. He will want to please you at all times. However, he is much like a child in many ways. There will be times when he becomes stubborn and mischievious and will be disobedient.

He will respond to various types of correction. However, for training purposes, the most effective correction will be a sharp NO spoken in a disapproving tone and accompanied with a quick sharp jerk on his leash.

Let us re-emphasize that you must have patience. Never swear or shout at your dog. This is an indication that you have lost control of yourself and when this occurs, you also lose control of your dog. You must know what you are doing if you want your dog to understand and respond to your commands.

Chapter 13

TRAINING SITE, OBSTACLE COURSE, EQUIPMENT NEEDS AND TRAINING SCHEDULE

SELECTION OF TRAINING SITE

Before starting a training program, you must select a training site. This should be in an obscure area not easily accessible to the general public. It should have a minimum area of five acres, fenced preferably with six foot fencing. It should have at least one building for the storage of equipment.

Much of the advance training, tracking and scent work will be done in large wooded areas not familiar to your dog, such as parks, farm areas, golf courses, etc.

OBSTACLE COURSE

An obstacle course will need to be constructed. This will aid you in teaching your animal to become a police dog. This area can also be used to exercise your dog since it is necessary, that he be exercised often to maintain top physical condition.

After you have completed his training you will need to give him a refresher course, putting him through his paces for approximately two hours each week. You should also take advantage of every opportunity while on duty to give your dog in-service training.

CONSTRUCTING THE OBSTACLE COURSE

If you are limited financially, you can build the needed obstacles from salvaged materials.

A good course will have hurdles, jumping ramp, walking logs, ladder and tunnel. You should consider the many different situations you may come in contact with in your particular locale and determine if you need others.

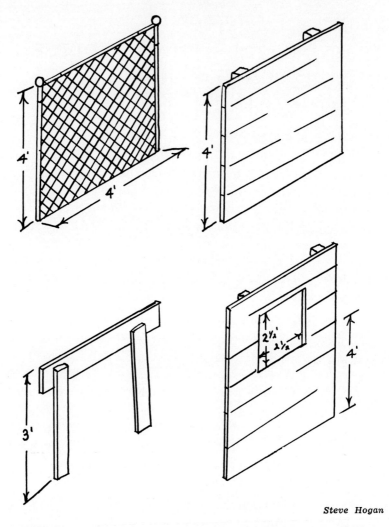

Steve Hogan

Fig. 4 Several types and sizes of hurdles should be constructed to simulate different situations with which your dog may be confronted. The framing of the hurdles should be buried in the ground at least 18 inches to insure steadiness.

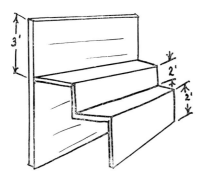

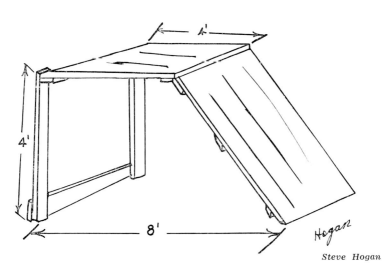

Steve Hogan

Fig. 5. Jumping ramps will teach your dog not to fear any place where you might take him. The frame of the upper illustration should be buried in the ground approximately 18 inches.

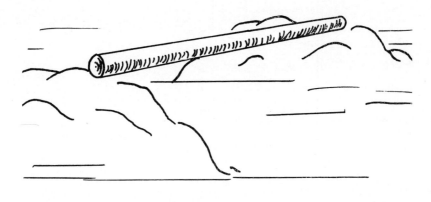

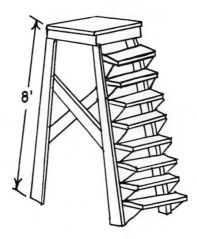

Jerry Pendry

Fig. 6. Walking logs and ladders will teach your dog to be sure-footed. The walking log should be fifteen to thirty feet in length. An old telephone pole or tree will make a good walking log.

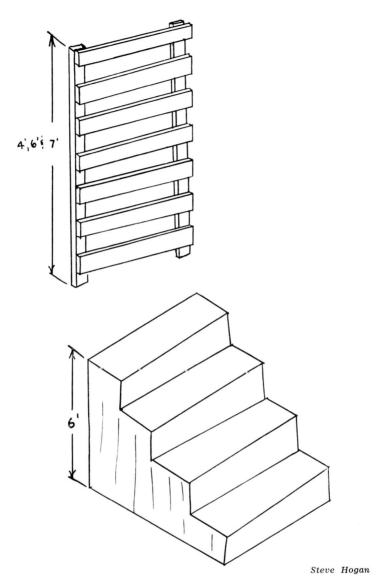

4', 6' & 7'

6'

Steve **Hogan**

Fig. 7. Walls and stairways will help teach your dog to climb. Construct climbing walls four, six and seven feet high. Once your dog learns to jump, it will be easy for him to learn to climb. The posts of the climbing walls should be buried in the ground at least 18 inches. It may be necessary to have an angular brace from the top of the high walls to the ground.

Construct a stairway a minimum height of six feet.

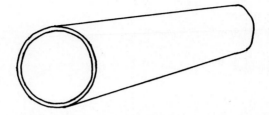

Jerry Pendry

Fig. 8. Tunnels will help teach your dog to crawl. A section of drainage pipe or several barrels placed together will serve as a good tunnel.

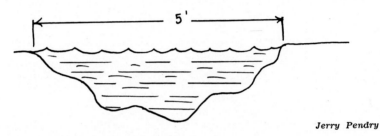

Jerry Pendry

Fig. 9. Constructing a water jump on your training site may not be feasible, but it is important that your dog not fear water. He can be trained at any stream or pond to jump or swim.

EQUIPMENT NEEDS

Equipment for Dog	Obstacle Course	Equipment for Handler
6 Foot Leash	Stairway	Attack Suit
20 Foot Leash	Window	Attack Sleeve
Leather Collar	Tunnel (Tubes)	38 Spl. Blank Revolver
Choke Chain	Water Jump	
Brush	Ramp	
Comb	Hurdles	
Harness	Walls	
Search & Signal Light	Walking Logs	
Feeding Bowl	Ladder	
Water Pail		
Muzzle		
2 Identification shields		

Leather leashes, leather collar, choke chain, brush, comb, feeding bowl, water pail and search and signal light may be purchased at any local pet supply. Harness can be made to order by local leather shop.

Equipment for the obstacle course must be erected.

The 38 spl. blank revolver may be purchased from any local sporting goods store.

EIGHT WEEKS' TRAINING COURSE

Basic Obedience (6 foot leash)	57 hours
Examination for control	2 hours
Total: 2 weeks	
Obedience Training (20 foot leash)	18 hours
Advanced Obedience Training (off leash)	7 hours
Apprehension and Agitation (crowd control)	27 hours
Examination for control	2 hours
Total: 3 weeks	
Transportation Training	8 hours
Tracking, Building Search, Retrieving	57 hours
Guarding prisoner, Apprehension of running prisoner	30 hours
Graduation	1 hour
Total: 3 weeks	

NOTE: Due to wide range of intelligence of animals, this program may have to be accelerated or decelerated for individual cases.

Chapter 14

BASIC AND ADVANCED
OBEDIENCE TRAINING

When training your dog, you must have his complete, undivided attention in order to obtain maximum results.

It is important that you only use a choke collar on your dog during obedience training. Never deviate from this pattern because it is necessary that your dog associate obedience work with the choke collar. When this collar is placed on the dog, he knows he must be obedient.

The choke collar is a chain-type collar that has a large ring on each end of the chain. The size of the collar to be used will depend on the size of the dog's head. When you purchase one, it should fit snuggly over his head.

Teaching your Dog the Command "Heel"

Equipment Needs: choke collar and six foot leash.

Place the choke collar on your dog's neck. Attach the six foot leash to the collar. Remember at all times to keep the leash loose unless you are giving commands or correcting your dog.

One of the first and most important commands you will teach your dog is to HEEL. The importance connected with this command is that it will be your dog's first association with correction and command obedience. The manner in which he learns that all is not play will be determined by your thoroughness, patience and understanding.

The position of the dog at HEEL is at your left side with your dog facing forward, his shoulder even with your left knee. After placing the dog in the HEEL position, step off on

Fig. 10. Command "Heel" Position.

your left foot. Give the command HEEL, snapping the leash which is attached to the choke collar at the same time. Repeat this action each time the dog tries to leave the HEEL position.

When you execute a turn during the first few lessons, the dog will continue walking in a straight line. When he does this, you snap the leash with a light pull toward the HEEL position which will cause him to return to the proper position.

If your dog hesitates and hangs back when walking at HEEL position, repeat the action of snapping the leash and pulling him forward or the right turn can be made to bring him back into position.

If he pulls forward, snap the leash pulling him back or make the reverse turn to bring him into position.

Be very firm but also understanding and never be too quick to make correction. But, when you do, make it a decisive one.

THE COMMAND "STAND"

When teaching your dog to STAND, especially if he has a tendency to sit down each time you stop, give a snap to the choke chain or leash, using the left hand to raise the hind-quarters to the STAND position, at the same time giving the command STAND· It is important here that you not move your feet since movement will confuse your dog.

THE COMMAND "SIT"

When first teaching your dog to SIT, he is also in HEEL position. You will take the leash in the left hand just above the choke chain, place the right hand on the rump of the dog, give the command SIT, giving a firm pull upward on the leash with the left hand and pushing the rump of the dog down with the right hand to a SIT position. Use downward, backward motion with the right hand as you give the command SIT. This exercise should be practiced until the dog SITS on command.

THE COMMAND "STAY"

Once your dog is thoroughly familiar with what it means to be obedient and is familiar with the commands HEEL, SIT and STAND, you will teach him the command STAY.

Place your dog in the HEEL position and give him the command SIT. With the leash in your left hand, place your right hand in front of the dog's nose with a firm snap on the choke chain, bring your right hand in front of the dog's nose and give the command STAY.

When you pull on the chain, pull backward and bring the right hand in front of his nose, give the command STAY, walk forward leaving the dog in the SIT-STAY position.

Fig. 11. Command "Sit" Position.

Fig. 12. Command "Stand-stay" Position.

At first, the dog will want to continue in a HEEL position, walking with you. Therefore, do not move far away and at the first sign of the dog breaking the STAY position, repeat the same action. It might be necessary for you to lightly tap his nose with your right hand and use a little more force on the choke chain until he is thoroughly familiar with the command STAY.

Use the command STAY when you have your dog in the SIT, DOWN or STAND positions.

Any time you place your dog in the STAY position, at the first sign of his breaking the position, you must correct him by giving the admonition NO followed by the command STAY, placing your hand in front of you, gesturing with the palm forward.

If the dog does break, you immediately put him back in the *exact position* and as near to the *exact spot* you had him, giving the same gesture and the command STAY.

In the first lessons, never place your dog in the STAY position for more than a few minutes or move too great a distance from him until he has thoroughly learned the STAY position. Repeat the exercise, leaving him a little longer in the STAY position and moving a greater distance from him. This is repeated, leaving him for a longer period and your moving a greater distance from him each time.

Remember that it is much easier for the dog if he is to be left in the STAY position for any length of time to be in the DOWN position. He will be less apt to break the STAY position if he is at DOWN.

THE COMMAND "DOWN"

As your dog increases in his ability to respond to the commands HEEL, SIT, STAND and STAY, you will teach him the command DOWN.

Take the six-foot leash which is attached to the choke chain in your left hand, placing your dog in the HEEL SIT position. Run the leash under your left foot between the heel and sole of the shoe. This will provide freedom of movement of the leash.

Fig. 13. Command "Down" Position.

Raise your left foot approximately six to twelve inches off the ground, give the command DOWN, pulling the leash up with your left hand and stepping down with the left foot giving a forward, downward gesture with your right hand. This will pull the dog's head and neck to the ground.

During the first few lessons, the dog's hindquarters will probably remain up. You will have to place your right hand on his hindquarters and push down, giving the command DOWN-STAY. Repeat this procedure until your dog responds

without resistance to a tap of the left foot and the command
DOWN.

Fig. 14. Command "Down-stay" Position.

Each time he responds to a command and executes it properly, praise him generously. However, do not praise him until
after the exercise has been completed. It is important to remember when you are putting your dog through an exercise
that has more than one phase never praise him for any one
part of the exercise but wait until it has been entirely completed. *Remember, his only reward is praise.*

COMMANDS AT A DISTANCE

When your dog is thoroughly responding to commands
at the HEEL position, give him the command SIT-STAY, leaving
him in this position. Walk away from your dog then face him,
holding the leash in your left hand. Give the dog the command DOWN-STAY with the gesture of the right hand at waist
level, a forward, downward motion and a tap of the left foot.
If the dog fails to respond, step in quickly, putting your left
foot on the leash stepping hard, pulling his head and neck to
the ground.

When he is familiar with this exercise, then proceed to the
SIT-STAY command, giving the gesture with the right hand, an

upward, forward motion. If he fails to respond, with the leash in your left hand, pull upward until he does respond properly.

Go on to the STAND-STAY command. If he fails to obey, step in quickly with the leash in your left hand, jerk upward, placing your right hand under his hindquarters lift up and give the command STAND-STAY. Repeat until he executes it properly.

THE COMMAND "COME"

Most dog trainers refer to this command as "recall dog." Place your dog in HEEL position giving him the command SIT-

Fig. 15. Command "Recall Dog" Position.

STAY. Walk to the end of the six foot leash and face your dog. Call your dog by name and give the command COME.

During the first few exercises, it will be necessary for you to jerk the leash with the needed force to make the dog respond, leading him to a position directly in front of and facing you. Give the command SIT-STAY, jerking up on the leash and giving the upward, forward motion with the right hand.

Then give the command HEEL making the dog come to HEEL position from the right side behind your back to your left leg.

JUMPS AND HURDLES

Most German Shepherds can jump and climb a three-foot hurdle or wall, but you need to teach your dog to do it on command. During the first lessons, your dog will be very awkward because this is something entirely new, but he will enjoy this training.

He must run from the HEEL position to your front and jump on the command HUP. After completing the jump, he then returns to the HEEL position. Your Shepherd will learn to jump hurdles to a height of five feet without too much difficulty.

He must learn to climb the six and seven foot walls. He does this by jumping as high on the wall as he can, catching the top of the wall with his front feet and legs. He then scrambles over the rest of the way.

During the beginning lessons, you should use hurdles that are low enough for your dog to step over and use this hurdle only until he responds to the command HUP.

Place the dog at HEEL position. Approach the hurdle at a fast walk. Step over with your left foot first, giving the command HUP. If the dog hesitates, pull on the leash and coax him over the hurdle. When the dog jumps over the hurdle, step away and give the command HEEL.

Gradually raise the height of the hurdle until the dog is jumping to an approximate height of five feet.

To teach your dog to climb the climbing wall, approach the wall at a run from the HEEL position. Give the command HUP. He will jump as high as possible, catch the top of the wall with his front legs and scramble over the rest of the way.

THE COMMAND "CRAWL"

Place your dog in DOWN-STAY at HEEL position. Take the leash with your left hand just above the choke chain. Lie down on the right side of your dog. Pull forward and downward on the leash with your left hand and give the command CRAWL. It will be necessary for you to crawl along beside your dog until he has learned to execute the command properly.

Do not tire your dog with this exercise. It is a difficult one for him to execute. At the first indication of your dog making an effort to crawl, praise him generously.

WALKING POLE, RAMPS, LADDERS AND STAIRWAYS

Teaching your dog to walk across the walking pole, climb ramps, ladders or stairs is not a difficult lesson. It is merely a process of leading him across or up a ramp or ladder until he becomes unafraid and sure-footed. Then, let him lead you.

Obstacle course training is very exhilarating to your dog if it is taught in the proper manner. Use it as an alternate to the DOWN, SIT, HEEL, STAND and STAY commands since these lessons are very depressing to your dog. However, obstacle training is very tiring and each exercise should be practiced just a few times each session, never allowing him more than three or four jumps before giving him the necessary rest and relaxation.

Since training is tiring and in many instances depressing to your dog, at the end of each session you should rough-house and play with him and allow him to romp and have the freedom to do as he wants for a little while. It is important to close each training session by leaving your dog in a happy frame of mind.

At the close of each training session, and before the play

time, put your dog through an exercise in which he excels in order that you can praise him generously. But, *never praise him if he does not honestly deserve it.*

TRANSPORTING

Teaching a German Shepherd to ride in an automobile requires little effort. The only problem that may arise is car sickness. When this develops, reduce the speed of the car and check to see if this will correct it. This problem should eliminate itself.

Place your dog at HEEL position. Walk him to the right side of the automobile or the rear of the station wagon, which ever type vehicle is used. Give the command SIT-STAY. Open the door you want him to enter and give the command HUP. Always make your dog enter and exit the vehicle from the same door or window and in the same way. Never allow him to enter an automobile until commanded.

ADVANCED OBEDIENCE TRAINING

Advanced obedience is putting your dog through all the exercises you have taught him and is done while he is off leash.

This is an important phase of his training and will develop the discipline necessary if you are to utilize your dog's ability effectively as a police dog.

THE SECRET OF TRAINING IS TO BE CONSISTENT. *WORK EVERY DAY.*

Chapter 15

AGITATION AND ATTACK TRAINING

Equipment Needs: Leather collar, protective sleeve, protective suit, small switch or stick.

An important factor in agitation and attack training is the man who plays the roll of the agitator. He must build self-confidence in the dog by acting afraid and backing away every time the dog makes an aggressive move toward him. The dog must feel that he is the winner in every instance during attack training.

Agitation is the process of teasing the dog to the point he tries to bit the agitator. The agitator wears a protective sleeve so the dog will actually have something to bite.

In all phases of attack training, teach the dog to attack the arm. This will accomplish the job that needs to be done and yet prevent serious injury in an attack.

The agitator will use a small switch or stick to irritate and make the dog angry so he will try to bite. It is important that the agitator never hit or strike the dog during his training to the degree that it will hurt him. If this is allowed, it will cause the dog to lose confidence in himself and risks breaking his spirit.

Keep in mind the aggressiveness you build in your dog during agitation training will determine his degree of alertness while on duty.

Remove the choke collar from your dog and replace it with a leather collar. This will be classified as the dog's work collar. It will be the only one used in attack training. It will also be the only one used while he is on duty. The choke chain collar will still be used off-duty for exercising and when basic obedience is the only requirement.

The dog is never to be agitated in the absence of his handler.

Agitation training is best done in groups. There are two methods of agitation discussed in this chapter. They are line follow agitation and circle agitation.

LINE FOLLOW

The handlers and dogs line up in single file spaced approximately fifteen to twenty feet apart. The agitator stations himself approximately twenty-five feet from the line and directly in front of the first dog and handler.

The only equipment the agitator will need is a switch or small stick. This will be used to agitate the dogs.

One at a time, the dog handlers will bring their dog toward the agitator. The agitator will make aggressive movements toward the dog and handler. When he does, the handler gives the command WATCH HIM. The agitator then acts afraid and moves slowly away from them. When the handler overtakes and is close enough, the agitator takes the switch and strikes the dog lightly across the chest area. He does this in such a way that it will cause the dog to make an aggressive move toward him. When the dog tries to bite, the agitator immediately backs off. The dog is not permitted to bite at this time.

The handler then turns his dog, walking him away from the agitator, praising and petting the animal,

This should be repeated three or four times in each session.

CIRCLE AGITATION

The purpose of circle agitation is to create a psychological chain reaction in the dogs. Dogs, much like people, like to be recognized and they do not like to be excelled. When they see other dogs acting aggressive toward the agitator, they will want to do the same.

Circle agitation is particularly effective when dogs are slow to attack.

The dogs and handlers will form a circle allowing approximately fifteen feet between each team. The agitator will station himself in the center of the circle with a small switch in his hand. The diameter of the circle will be determined by the number of dogs being trained.

The dogs and handlers in unison will move toward the agitator and he will immediately begin to act aggressive. Each handler will give the command WATCH HIM. The agitator will move slowly toward the dogs using the switch to strike them on the chest area lightly, then back away and act afraid.

As the circle gets smaller, the handlers shorten the leash until they are holding the dog by the leather collar. After a few moments of agitation, the handlers will give the command OUT and return to their original positions.

At this time, the agitator puts the protective sleeve on his arm. As the handler and dog approach the agitator, he becomes aggressive toward the dog. The handler gives the command WATCH HIM. When the dog gets close enough to the agitator, he will use the switch to irritate the dog and make him

Fig. 16. Individual Agitation With Protective Sleeve.

attack. The handler will then give the command GET HIM.

The handler will permit his dog to bite the protective sleeve. After the dog has taken hold of the sleeve with his mouth, the handler gives the command OUT and returns the dog to his original position, praising and petting him as he re-positions.

This is repeated by each dog and handler three or four times each session.

CROWD CONTROL

After your dog has been taught to attack, teaching crowd control will not be a problem. After being trained, your dog will alert and attack any person who makes an act of aggression. You will notice during the training sessions that when the agitator ceases to resist, the dog will automatically stop his attack.

Place your dog at HEEL position. The simulated crowd should be several men in a straight line, shoulder to shoulder, each facing the dog. Work your dog parallel to the line.

One at a time, the men as agitators, make an aggressive move toward the dog. Give the command WATCH HIM, then the agitator ceases his aggressive action. If your dog fails to alert, the agitator will use a small switch striking the dog on the chest area lightly. Once the dog attacks, the agitator ceases resistance. Give the command OUT and praise your dog.

The agitators then, all at one time, start toward the dog making aggressive actions. Give the command WATCH HIM. When the dog attacks, the group should cease all aggressive action. Give the command OUT and praise the dog.

APPREHENSION OF RUNNING SUSPECTS

In this exercise, the agitator will need to wear the protective suit to prevent the possibility of being severely bitten on an unprotected area of the body. Your dog will be off-leash and will not be as easily controlled.

Place your dog at HEEL position. Approach the agitator. The agitator will become aggressive toward the dog. Give the command WATCH HIM and when the agitator approaches close enough, give the command GET HIM, allowing your dog to bite the arm of the protective suit. The agitator will then cease resistance and you give the command OUT. At this time, praise and pet your dog.

Order the agitator to place his hands over his head. The agitator ignores this order and starts to run. After the order is given to halt and the order disregarded, release your dog and give him the command GET HIM.

After the dog has caught the agitator, there should be a brief struggle between the agitator and dog. The agitator will then cease all resistance. Give your dog the command OUT, snap the leash on his collar and lead him away from the agitator while praising and petting him.

GUARDING PRISONERS AND PROTECTING HANDLER

Have your dog at HEEL position as you approach the agitator who will make aggressive moves toward the dog. Give the command WATCH HIM. The agitator will cease all resistance and you order the agitator to place his hands above his head.

Lead your dog approximately fifteen feet away from the agitator, place him in a SIT-STAY position, giving him the command WATCH HIM.

Walk to the agitator, never at any time blocking the view between the agitator and your dog. The agitator will be standing perfectly still with his hands over his head. Begin to search the agitator, keeping one eye on your dog and the other on the agitator. It is important that your dog maintain his position during the search when there is no resistance from the agitator.

After your dog has executed the command SIT-STAY-WATCH HIM while you are searching a would-be prisoner (agitator) then the agitator, while you are still searching him, will turn and strike you on the shoulder. This being an aggressive move, the dog will immediately come to your aid and attack the agitator. After a few moments struggle, the agitator will cease to resist. Give the command OUT and lead your dog to one side as you praise and pet him.

GUN FIRE

It is essential that your dog not be afraid of gun fire. A dog that is gun shy is worthless in a situation where a suspect is armed.

If your dog evidences shyness to gun fire, you should spend as much time as possible to eliminate this tendency. Have someone fire a small caliber weapon from a distance while you talk to your dog in a soft tone of voice. This will comfort and reassure him if he is frightened. Decrease the distance as your dog evidences less nervousness.

Frequently during attack training, the agitator should fire a small caliber blank weapon.

Another method that has proven effective is used at feeding time. When you feed your dog, fire a small caliber blank weapon in the kennel area. If your dog runs into his house and tries to hide, take the food away and do not allow him to eat. Repeat the same procedure the next day.

It is absolutely necessary that a dog in police service be taught to attack against gun fire without hesitation.

Never allow anyone to pet your dog. He is to know that he has one master and one master only.

Chapter 16

TRACKING AND SCENT TRAINING

Training a dog to track and do scent work is a process of teaching him to distinguish certain scents . . . more specifically, the scent you want him to follow or find.

RETRIEVING

Retrieving is one of the first steps in teaching your dog to distinguish a particular scent. With your dog at HEEL position, the leash in your left hand, you will first teach your dog to take and hold an object. It is important that the object used have a smooth surface and not be hard for your dog to hold or one that would irritate his mouth.

Drop the leash on the ground and stand on it with your left foot to prevent the dog moving from his position. Take the object, which can be a small block of wood, force the dog's mouth open and place the block of wood in it. Place your hands on top of and beneath your dog's mouth forcing it closed as you give the command TAKE IT.

If he attempts to drop the block of wood, force his mouth closed again, patting him firmly under the chin with your right hand and give the command TAKE IT.

When he executes this properly and takes the block of wood on command, praise him. However, if he struggles, use force to hold his mouth closed and tap him under the chin more firmly with the repeated command TAKE IT.

To begin the next step in teaching your dog to retrieve, take the block of wood and hold it just a few inches in front of his mouth. Give him the command TAKE IT. If he hesitates, with the leash in your left hand pull him toward the object, forcing him to go forward and take the object. When he executes this properly, praise him.

Increase the distance between the article and your dog, each time placing it lower to the ground until he is moving approximately four or five feet and reaching down within six inches of the ground and taking the object.

When this is properly executed, take the block of wood and throw it to the ground about ten feet in front of you. Then give the command GO TAKE IT. After executing properly, increase the distance until your dog retrieves the article on command.

Have someone stack blocks of the same general size approximately fifteen feet from you and your dog. Take one of the blocks, put a mark on it so you will be able to determine which one it is, throw the block of wood into the pile and give the command GO TAKE IT. Since this block of wood will have your scent on it, your dog will immediately seek it out and find it.

Each time your dog retrieves an article, have him come to HEEL position and hold the article in his mouth until you give him the command GIVE.

TRACKING

Equipment Needs: Harness and twenty-foot leash.

After your dog learns to retrieve, he will be aware that he must distinguish scents on command. Tracking is not a difficult exercise to teach but one that will take a great deal of practice, time and patience.

Put the harness on the dog. Run the twenty-foot leash through the ring which is located between the front quarters underneath the dog and attach it to the collar. This will tend to keep your dog's head down closer to the scent.

During the first few lessons, it will be helpful if the track layer is someone your dog has associated with, preferably one of the agitators.

The track layer will play an important part in teaching

your dog to track, for in the beginning lessons, he must lay a track that will not be difficult for your dog to follow. It will be good for him to drag his feet while laying the track during the first lessons.

The first exercise in tracking is a straight trail with the wind blowing into your dog's face. The track layer will move to the starting point which should be designated by a stake or a mark. He will scuff the ground thoroughly with his feet, then start walking in a straight line, placing a stake about every twenty-five feet. These stakes will aid you in keeping your dog on the right trail at all times.

During the first lessons, the trail layer will go only a short distance, then hide. At the half-way point of the trail, he will drop some article which will have his scent on it.

Place your dog at HEEL position, take him to the starting point and put him in DOWN-STAY in the exact area scuffed by the trail layer. Leave your dog at DOWN-STAY for approximately one minute. This will give him the opportunity to thoroughly detect the scent of the trail layer. Then give the command FIND HIM.

At first, it may be necessary for you to guide or even lead your dog, but by all means, keep him on the correct trail. When he is on the trail, give him vocal encouragement.

Never let your dog be distracted by other animals. Never let him stop to relieve himself. He must give his undivided attention to tracking. If he does stop, jerk the leash and correct him by giving the admonition NO in a firm voice. He will realize he did something wrong. Lead him back to the trail and the moment he responds, give him added words of encouragement.

If your dog hesitates and acts as though he has lost the trail, talk to him, give him words of encouragement, allow him time to move about keeping him in the area of the trail. Many times he will find the trail himself.

At the half-way point, encourage the dog. Make sure he finds the article that was dropped by the trail layer. Give him the command TAKE IT and let him bring it to you. Give him praise and pet him generously before putting him back on the trail with the command FIND HIM.

As your dog approaches the trail layer, he will begin to alert and become excited. At this time, encourage him and give him the command FIND HIM. The trail layer should step out then and offer no resistance. Praise and pet your dog.

Wind direction will play a definite part in trail work. Exercise your dog in tracking straight trails with the wind in all directions. After the dog has learned to track a straight trail, introduce him to turns.

With the introduction of turns, it is important that the trail layer leave a stake when and where he turns so you will know where turns were made and be able to guide your dog if it becomes necessary.

Wind direction will definitely play a part in the way your dog trails. When he approaches a turn, depending upon the wind direction, he may cut a corner. He may completely eliminate a portion of the trail and cross over if the trail has been reversed and is parallel.

When approaching a corner, never praise your dog or give him words of encouragement. In an effort to please you, he may want to continue in a straight line. If he does want to continue in a straight line, allow him to circle and he will probably be able to pick up the trail again on his own. If he does not, give him the needed assistance to put him on the right trail.

One of the most important rules in the exercise of tracking is to never let your dog give up without finding the trail layer.

There are many things to know and understand if you want your dog to trail successfully.

Disturb the trail as little as possible.

As you follow your dog, motion and noise should be kept at a minimum.

Never allow anyone to walk along with you unless it is absolutely necessary.

Never think your dog is not trailing because he holds his head high. During the morning hours, the dog's head will be held high because the air is rising. During the evening, his head will be held low because the air is heavy.

It will be necessary for the other officers in your Department to be educated to protect and preserve the area they want a trained dog to trail. Any items that may have belonged to the suspect should not be touched by another individual. This will give the dog a definite advantage and will increase the possibility of catching the suspect.

SCENT WORK

This will be teaching your dog to seek out and find people who are hiding in areas or terrain such as woodland, high grass, small buildings, lake areas, etc.

In scent work, your dog will not be following a trail. He will respond to any strong scent other than that of his handler.

Use the twenty-foot leash and harness and take your dog to the area where the suspect is hiding. If possible, enter the area with the wind blowing in your dog's face. Give the command FIND HIM and allow your dog the freedom of the leash to rove in front of you.

Many times a dog will alert first because he hears a noise. This is especially true when the wind is blowing the scent away from him.

When your dog picks up a scent other than your own, he will react, becoming very alert and aggressive and take you in a straight line toward the scent. Depending on the dog, he will begin to growl or bark. When your dog does alert and pull on the leash, praise and pet him, giving him words of encouragement and allow him to take you in the direction of the scent.

When your dog gets within a few feet of the suspect (who is your agitator) the suspect will jump out making threatening gestures. Give the command WATCH HIM. If the agitator ceases resistance, praise your dog. However, if the agitator should resist, give the command GET HIM. Allow your dog to bite the protective sleeve. After a brief struggle, resistance should cease. *Remember your dog is to be the winner in all exercises.*

BUILDING SEARCH

After your dog has been trained to alert, seek out and find the agitator by scent or noise in open fields, ditches, trees or tunnels, the searching of a building is a relatively easy exercise to teach.

The agitator, dressed in the protective suit, conceals himself in the building. Having an instinctive curiosity and suspicion, your dog will have a desire to search when he is taken into a building. The command FIND HIM is given.

For a few lessons, the agitator should be concealed in such a place that your dog can easily locate him. When your dog alerts on the agitator's scent, he should be praised and petted.

When your dog is within a few feet of the concealed agitator, the agitator should jump out and make threatening gestures. Give the command WATCH HIM. This exercise should be repeated numerous times with the agitator being concealed in various locations causing your dog to search with an increasing degree of dilligence.

Make variations in your exercise. Sometimes have the agitator resist. When he does, give your dog the command GET HIM. After he has taken hold of the protective sleeve, give the command OUT. You may also want to practice the exercise by letting the agitator run from your dog and allow your dog to apprehend him.

When in the actual search of a building while on duty, always remember to keep your dog on-leash until it has been determined whether the intruder has just cause to be in the building. Many times, investigation of burglary reports reveal that an owner or employee has entered the building after hours for good reason. This bit of caution will prevent an innocent party being attacked by your dog.

Dogs will never replace men. They are only supplemental

and make the service you provide to your community more effective. In police departments that attempt to replace men with dogs, the program failed.

Do not make the mistake of trying to use dogs in every phase of police work. They are not suited for all areas, but will excel in such specialized jobs as building search, tracking, handler protection, crowd control, riots, guard work, etc.

A working dog is an alert dog. If a department uses too many dogs for job demands, the animals will not be active enough to keep them alert.

Your dog has now been trained to do a specific job. He will be a credit to you personally and to your entire department.

In order to maintain his efficiency, it is important that the benefits gained during the initial training period be continually developed. To insure a high standard of efficiency, both you and your dog should be given a refresher training period each week. This training should be under the supervision of your Department. Much of the efficiency of your dog depends upon you, his handler. Unless the lessons and exercises are constantly applied and developed, the animal will lose his sharpness and will not do the job he was originally trained to do.

INDEX

85

Protective ability, 43
Protective sleeve arm, 73, 82
Protection
  of officer, 8
  of handler, 75-76
Protective suit, 74, 75, 82
Protozoa, 33
Psychological
  effect, 8
  advantage, 8
  approach, 5
Public
  acceptance, 6, 10, 17
  funds, 8
  demonstration, 45
  participation, 10, 17
  relations, 8, 43-45

Qualities of dog, 49
Qualification of dog, 17
Questionnaire, 18

Rabies, 31
Radio, 7
Rapport between handler and dog, 26
Records, 9, 36-42
Refresher course, 53
Relationship between dog and
    handler, 21
Release by owner, 18
Replacement, 9
Responsibility, 15, 32
Retrieving
  exhibit, 43
  training, 77-78
Role of dog in police work, 8
Rules for good feeding, 28
Roundworms, 32

Safety
  dog, 24
  emphasis, 44
  human, 36
Salary for handler, 6, 7

Sanitary conditions, 30, 32
Scent training, 77-83
Searching, 82
Selective enforement, 39
Selection
  of dogs, 6, 9, 17-20
  of handlers, 14-16
Self-discipline, 14
Sensitivity, 50
Sex of dog, 18
Shock, 35
Sleep, 21
Smell, sense of, 48, 50
Snakebite, 35
Standards, 17, 18
Stool, 30
Stud purposes, 13
Supplement, 29
Symptoms of sick dog, 33

Tactical procedures, 9
Teeth, 28, 29
Temperament, 18
Time schedule, 7
Toenails, 27-28
Tracking training, 77-83
Trail, 78, 79, 80, 81
Training
  of dogs, 6, 47-83
  equipment, 38
  record, 38
  three types, 47
  in-service, 53
  course, 59
  site, 39, 53-59
  follow-up, 83
Transportation of dog, 9, 24-25

Uniform, 15

Vehicle
  construction, 24-25
  entry, 70

M.